Joyful Annotations to the World Outside

Joyful Annotations to the World Outside

Poems by

Carol Sadtler

Cover design by Shay Culligan
Cover image by Hecate Mu on Unsplash
Author photo by Benoit Cortet

ISBN: 978-1-63980-758-1

Kelsay Books
502 South 1040 East, A-119
American Fork, Utah 84003
Kelsaybooks.com

to my family, with love and admiration

Acknowledgments

Thank you to the following publications, in which versions of these poems previously appeared:

Bangalore Review: "In the Jardin Etno-botánico"
Big City Lit: "Solstice, Lake Shore Drive"
Hartskill Review: "Hymn to Her," "No Such Thing as Angels"
The Keeping Room Magazine: "Infinity Pond"
Liminal Spaces: "The words gone out"
Maine Review: "Up to My Ankles" as "Tide Pool"
One Art by: "Loggerheads"
Pacific Review: "Gracia"
Red Wolf Journal: "To a Persian New Year"
Rhino Review: "Praise Him"
Rise Up Review: "National Gallery: Portrait #44," "America's Presidents Tour"
River Heron Review: "Letter from a Bird Mother to Her Daughter"
Shadowgraph Quarterly: "Walking Latham Road"
Sky Island Journal: "Today I'm Something I Have Never Been Before"
Spank the Carp: "Slow Time"
Speckled Trout Review: "Retouch"
Thimble Literary Magazine: "At the Last"
The Tishman Review: "Wherever I May Find You"

Many thanks to Gail Goepfert for years of generously sharing her expertise and encouragement, and to Ralph Hamilton for connecting me with *RHINO* Poetry and Plumb Line Poets when I returned to Chicago. To both of you, thank you for your careful editorial help with this manuscript.

To the Plumb Line Poets, thank you for letting me join you as a late-comer years ago. I value your astute comments, hilarity and support each time we meet.

To my spouse, Jackie Taylor, boundless thanks for the life we have made together, including our ongoing and innumerable discussions about words.

To my long-time friends, Carol Brice and Donna Lausier, thank you for assuring me years ago that you enjoyed my poems—and that other people would, too.

Contents

Letter from a Bird Mother

to her daughter

How we fly in patterns to the slant
        of a season's light. Seems I never
wing my true height though
            every fresh wind urges my heart
            to thrum its own trajectory.

Takes me most of a life to know
        that the meek do not inherit
that the arrow sticks the dove
            while those that draw the bow score
            both the laurels and the spoils.

In this earthy thicket the blackbird
        flares his wings and struts his red
shoulder pads as the dove
            covers her eggs with dun-colored feathers
            and murmurs lamentations.

I nourish your downy self, show you
        how to preen
        damaged feathers
wheel across a Blossom Moon
            ride the windshifts
            of your own wild choices.

Wherever I May Find You

You groan as you roll in the bed tonight. Our long bones align,
parallel, yet impossibly connected; how we turn and turn
in that paradox.

The man in a Wisconsin campground who tried to make sense
of us—two tall women in a pup tent. "What are you? A couple of
. . . schoolteachers?"

There were two coffees, two beignets, lying side by side
that New Orleans morning when we wished two daughters
into being;

When I told my father, the lines in his forehead creased in
contradiction: "You're working girls. Who's going to take care
of your children?"

There were so many years of filling out forms that never fit
our family, crossing out father writing mother
twice;

We crossed a continent to find a place that would marry us,
choosing whose name fits the line labeled "groom"
in Vancouver;

I remember that your sister's spine fractured with the slightest
strain, and how the metal pins in my mother's hips glowed
in her x-rays;

In my dream, our bones shatter; fragments
are laid in the ground, then dissolve, and mingle
in earth, in air.

My Father the Lifeguard

His hawk-like nose, his corn-fed frame—my dad
wades in chlorine water with five-year-olds
as the country club moms sip their sodas. Blue-lipped
from morning chill the little kids cling to his hairy
arm while others lean back to float—trust his wide-spread
hand and the liquid lift of water.

Big figure at East High in his school-year job—everybody
knows The Coach. Summers he makes what he can—
boasts to us about his day at The Club. Says the big shots
who dine on the balcony admire his basketball wins
and the crew in the kitchen where he eats in the back
saves him the best cuts of meat.

Loggerheads

Her wide-stance waddle
her forward head with tiny
eyes—who would not
want to meet her
on the beach. Flippers

guided by the tides
and an ancient algorithm,
she mates in shallows, drags
her heavy carapace
ashore to birth new

generations begun
60 million years since—
only to be undone
by condos and chemicals

but for now, carretta carretta
let's swim in a watery
slipstream, my breaststroke

matching yours in your
warm lightgreen world
where we pretend
our children's children
will not miss this.

Walking Latham Road

Blackbird flashes
through the bright green cornstalks—
his piercing, full-throated trill
arresting me
on the hot asphalt
as all that rushes in
to fill me—

I dissolve in it—
that red
on a black wing.

Praise Him

with lines from Psalms 139:14

After she died I cut my hair.
Saw in the mirror my father or my brother.
"Not bad," I thought.
I am

more me than I have been since I was twelve,
standing on the shore with a towel around my neck,
hair wet from a cold swim,
looking sideways at the camera
like a tough guy—innocent,
with only a hint of fear in my face
about the woman I will be required
to become.

Now the critics are quiet.
How long before I seize
my own life? Shake it,
explode in it. Maybe now,
for I am
fearfully and wonderfully made.

In the Jardín Etno-botánico

Snaking through mesquite
       and saguaro—a long line
of jibber-jabber, pink-
       necked tourists muffle
the words of the Zapotec
       guide who shows us
a geometry of amaranth
       and maize

we have always planted
in sacred shapes and symbols

A couple is squabbling
       and teenagers flirt
as we troop through
       a greenhouse of orchids
and damp

we capture the rain
as we always have—and cool
in summer with geo-thermal

Outside in the healing
garden, she picks a leaf
from a flowering plant—
crushing delicate green
with her fingers

smell this chepil—
a seasoning and vegetable
my people have eaten
for thousands of years

Folks wander and chat
        while she tells the old stories—
what flourished and what remains.
        Every time

she says—Oaxaca—
soft syllables float
from the back of her throat
then blossom and linger

Gracia

I.

For lo, the winter is past, that bosomy, grandmotherly
Sunday school teacher reads—the rain
is over and gone, though we children sit
in damp boots while the radiator steams
and colored ribbons stream from the
King James in her lap—joyful
annotations to the muddy world outside.

II.

Another time in another hemisphere
the streets are empty as the moon
I search for medicine in a city
of bare shelves and bombs
I pray to an ancient mother
for the baby I hold in my arms.
A cab pulls up—the driver knows
an all-night drugstore that has everything.

III.

Jacaranda blooms everywhere this Easter Week—
its pinks and lavenders softening stone
in the Zocalo. I visit the Black Christ
in the cathedral where pilgrims drop coins
and prayers. Sunlight suddenly catches
His torn flesh and mine
—and I gleam
in the same random beam.

Infinity Pond

lap upon lap, around and back
in sparkling aqua circles
our rhythmic kicks aerate
water into froth—arms dip
in synchrony—propelling joy

we are beautiful in our blue and green
swimsuits—my younger sister and I
—like newly-hatched sunfish—know
the wriggle and glide in the shallows
—the ease of a watery world

after your diagnosis you refuse
your dis-ease—now the impetus
to heal with elemental cures—
renew your tissue with herbs
and breath and yes—water

—Iceland's Golden Circle—we dream
to balm the present with this magic
tour from pond to river to ocean—warm
milky mineral waters—then the shock
of Reykjavik's winter sea

lap upon lap, around and back
in sparkling aqua circles
our rhythmic kicks aerate
water into froth—arms dip
in synchrony—propelling joy

Last One Standing

We climb with shallow breaths
        as the road twists up to her
while winds stir arsenic dust
        from the Salt Lake basin

We blame a history of profiteers
        for what little good it does—
farmers and miners and builders
        working land to death

But here she stands—this hickory
        her bosom slashed by lightning
yet still rooted
        twined with burnished grasses

She sips what little water melts
        from snowy peaks above
watches as her valley
        sere and thirsty—whirls away

Hymn to Her

Ancient mother you send
no solicitations but the orange glow
of maples against grimy walls
of churches and prisons.

Mother of us all you
suckle the hungry—carry
corpses on your back to graves
filled by war and neglect.

Your compassion
my bridge
from irony to meaning—
I accept
no substitutes for your
earthy embrace.

Mother and maker, you shoot
beauty across the sky
—take clay
to shape animals, stars, mountains,
and us.

Fragile figures fired
in hot coals
glazed with dung
and smoke—
shiny with knowing
like your eyes.

Up to My Ankles

in this cold and salty
        tide pool

I tell its shelled inhabitants
        my woes:

You mollusks do not have
        to choose.

You sit complete
        and in community—

The sun shines
        or it doesn't—

The moon waxes
wanes
        disappears

The waves sweep in
        recede
return

        You ride out
You come back

Muckling onto the rock
        that sustains you

connected
        to the first waves
of the universe.

On shore—
we upright
sentient creatures

our soft selves
whorled inward
behind our armor

we scramble and scuffle
—kill to find
our destinies

while you rest
        in the rhythms
of yours.

At the End of the Day

No one sees me you say
             and I wonder which self
you mean them to see?

the heart that slashes
             or the one that soothes

your wily mind or
             innocent essence

your rigid discipline
             or your whimsy

I put on some Nina Simone
             her gravelly growl
rough and comforting

as sunset strikes scarlet
             berries in the Hawthorne
so sweet and lethal

the words gone out

with a line by W. S. Merwin

Heeding the poets, I sow
      milkweed and cornflowers
in my barren urban lot.
      They draw
           butterflies and children

Alice Walker roots herself in dirt—
      Like a tree she converts elements
to nutrients—nourishing her stories.
      She knows
         what sustains us

Adrienne Rich knows the ocean—
      draws sea air into her body
breathes poems out as lifeblood.
      She hopes
           there's still time

Merwin tends his island trees—
      decodes—transmits their warnings
while beaches shrink and drunken Zorba

      dances
         in the waves

To a Persian New Year

Twelve days after the equinox
      Sara sets out sprouting seeds for new life
apples for beauty, olives for love
      an egg, coins, sumac, vinegar
seven small bowls to bless the guests

The tea comes in tall glasses
      curved to fit our empty hands
These windowed walls 27 stories
      above the city diffuse a gray day
into light that softens our faces

Soothed by rosewater and hyacinth
      we sink into soft cushions
slough off past adversities and laugh
      as Mosen pours the wine
we toast Hafez, and ourselves

Prayer for Lucia at Four

You dream of sleeping overnight
      in the library—surrounded by books
you crack and consume
      as a squirrel gobbles peanuts

You seize new words and ideas
      as if they were candy
snatch each new tidbit
      like a bird grabs worms

You seek connection everywhere
      ask to be seen
while your innocent eyes scan
      for any friendly face

Your tender, singular self
      heart open to the world—
May a mother's songs and prayers
      carry you on

Today I'm Something I Have Never Been Before

I peel down blacktop back roads, fly by July-high cornstalks
and hayfields, away from my boring little town. Today
I am not my brother's keeper, not my mother's daughter, not
the one who does all the dishes. I turn on a dirt path, speed
up, hit teeth-rattling ruts. I look at my tanned, strong forearms.
I'm a pilot, adventurer, explorer. I run the whole show. I talk
back to the chirr of a red-winged blackbird. I pause to pick
Black-eyed Susans and Queen Anne's lace. I'm 10 years old. I
have a watch and a new bike. I am master of time and space

Retouch

Mother's mother or was it
mother's mother's mother
my mother wasn't sure which
but here's a photo—

a shadow face
obscured by her bonnet
a wraith of a woman
captured
in black and white
feeding chickens
on a West Texas plain—

hanging over us kids
in a heavy frame
while mother disappears
into the back bedroom
to tap herself
onto reams of yellow paper
with an old Remington

These boxes of paper
that photo left to me
when she passed
I spend years sifting
ochre from mud
learn to mix gold
with red and grief

with my brush
I stroke her face
a warrior's face
that bursts the frame.

In a Summer, Mourning

I wake early empty
        as a walnut shell
stale as an old cracker

A plain clay pot
        spills waterfalls
of small green leaves

Zinnias explode
        in scarlet and gold
and purple petals

I'm so tired of missing you
        the heft of last year
earns no place here

        a Monarch lands
                lightly sips nectar
        glides over the grass

to lose herself
        in a tangle
of Black-eyed Susans

No Such Thing as Angels

You sit at midnight making angels, practiced
fingers twisting fabric and crystals into gauzy
figures for fairs and galleries, as embers pop
in the quiet, as wood smoke drifts towards the sky,
as the Great Bear points to Arcturus.

You believe guardian angels attend you; I believe
they watched over you as you scrubbed floors
on your knees in the Quick Stop that winter you lost
your job, as you got up to care for your cancerous
friend, as you eased the waste from her dying
body with your hands when she grew too
weak to move—your earthy act of spirit;
no angel, no saint, no nurse could have done more.

You make angels, while I wonder if in the beginning
was the word and the word was spirit, or if the flesh
came first and learned to speak its yearning—or if
how it all went even matters.

Embers pop in the quiet, as smoke drifts towards
the sky, as the Great Bear points to Arcturus,
and the orange star cuts sideways through time.

Hitchcock Replay

A wild barking in the distance
a cacophony of crows swoops
roosts in the barren crown
of a craggy maple
startles some primal part in me
no tribal sage or fable to interpret
my unease—

I repeat this story to neighbors and friends
as we gather in flocks to speculate
hungry to substantiate what
we may or may not be
able to bear knowing

National Gallery: Portrait #44

"America's Presidents" Tour

I walk long halls where pale men hang
in formal shirts and ties—then suddenly a joyfulness
Hawaiian white jasmine, blue lilies from Africa
lush leaves and showy blossoms burst in the frame.
Centered and larger than life a long-limbed figure
sits forward and easy—arms folded
and elbows lightly on knees, his shins parallel
in reassuring symmetry while vines twine his ankles and feet
and gravity shadows his face—I look beneath brush strokes
—see dogged roots in soil
soured
by blood and history
push green life towards sunlight and air
as the earth cracks to create space for fresh images
in new frames—some garden always growing.

Slow Time

Takes hours to walk
the fields when I give
the dog her nose—

follow as she nuzzles
every green blade
that pokes from mud
and snow

—inhales
invisible clues
to steer her way—

pauses to tongue
a puddle in her path—
so I can notice

how high
bare branches
mirror

how water beads
drop sounds

I have
never heard.

At the last

she plants herself in the shadow
of the Wasatch Range—
not that she could still
clamber up the steep
trails to Gobbler's Knob—
but to recall the clear air
at the tree-line
and the snow.

Her arid valley holds
everything—two daughters—
one granddaughter—
the Oquirrh Mountains
and what is left
of the Great Salt Lake.

Her kitchen window frames
the sunrise as she rotates
a numbered block each day
in a hand-carved rosewood
calendar on the sill.

In her front room—spread
on calm white walls
and warm maple floors—
a traveler's colorful treasures.

Deep blue cushions comfort
her thinning form—
her mind still here.
She lives as always
for the sunsets—seeking
a panorama, not this
living room's stingy view—
she wants to blast the bricks
in the northwest corner
for a picture window.

Her hand-woven rug
a pictorial—with one
thin horizontal line
that runs from center
to edge—at the last—
an opening out

Solstice, Lake Shore Drive

The Queen of Spades looks up at me
from a chilly city sidewalk

I put her in my pocket—one stray
card with a two-faced queen—

At the end of this ragged year
before the longest night

Eight lanes of heavy metal boxes exhale
fumes north and south like always

and towers rise higher every year
as the tideline does.

Waning light reflects to gray
the lapping waves.

I lay the card back on the ground—
ask the west wind for a reading

About the Author

Born in Rockford, Illinois, Carol Sadtler earned a BA in English at Knox College and an MA in Comparative Literature at the University of Maine. She began to write poetry while she worked as a magazine editor and marketing communications writer for organizations in the Midwest and Eastern US.

She served as an assistant editor at *RHINO* and is a member of Plum Line Poets. Her poems and reviews appear in *River Heron Review, One Art, Sky Island Journal, Big City Lit, The Inflectionist, Rise Up, The Humanist, Pacific Review, RHINO,* and other publications. She lives in Chicago with her family.

www.ingramcontent.com/pod-product-compliance
Lightning Source LLC
Chambersburg PA
CBHW071115090426
42737CB00013B/2594